The Official Manchester City Football Club Annual 2005

Written by
David Clayton

For Jack Kelly – the bravest young Blue I've ever known

g

A Grange Publication

© 2004. Published by Grange Communications Ltd., Edinburgh,
under licence from Manchester City Football Club. Printed in the EU.

With special thanks to Manchester City photographer Edward Garvey

£6.99

ISBN 1-902704-76-2

Contents

Player of The Year
Shaun Wright-Phillips

There were several contenders for the coveted supporters award for Player of the Year but there was only ever going to be one winner - Shaun Wright-Phillips. The 22 year-old star was one of the few shining lights in what turned out to be a fairly disappointing season, but Wright-Phillips' form rarely dipped as he became many a fullback's worst nightmare.

He even won a place in the England squad when he was called up for the friendly in Sweden shortly before Euro 2004, but a badly-timed injury meant he had to settle for remaining on the bench, unfit to play. Many City fans felt he should have still been selected for the England squad that flew out to Portugal in the summer but no doubt he will feature in the World Cup 2006 qualifiers this season.

Wright-Phillips began the season with a goal against Total Network Solutions and in doing so became the second official scorer ever at the new stadium. As City roared out of the starting blocks, it was the form of the young England star that was one of the main driving forces of the side.

Yet it would be three months before he found the net again, but he did it with style, chipping the Bolton goalkeeper Jussi Jaaskelainen with a delightful lob to put the Blues level in a crucial game. He added another after the break but was then sent off for a second bookable foul! Quite a day!

He added another two goals two games later in the Coca Cola Cup but as City's form dipped, he managed just one more goal in 2003 – a terrific solo effort at Old Trafford. Of course, his game isn't just based on goals – he creates numerous chances and is one of the best defenders at the club. He can also dribble, shoot, cross and has exquisite control.

If the first half of the season had been good for Wright-Phillips, the second was even better. He scored an incredible last minute goal against Manchester United to complete a 4-1 win and he also scored a wonderful injury-time equaliser against Wolves to earn a vital point for the Blues.

Following his England call-up, he was voted runner-up in the prestigious PFA Young Player of the Year awards and ended the season in explosive style with a fantastic – you guessed it – last minute strike against Everton.

Modest as ever, he thanked his teammates for helping him win the Player of the Year award at City. This award was the fans' way of thanking him for all his efforts and never-say-die attitude. A real star!

Most teams would be happy to score eight goals without reply in the first two matches of the season and the Blues were no different. Okay, one of those games was against a non-League Welsh team, Total Network Solutions, but they still had to be beaten. That game, a UEFA Cup qualifier, was the first official match to be played at the City of Manchester Stadium and new arrival Trevor Sinclair's volley on 14 minutes was the first of five on the night.

The trip to Charlton Athletic for the Premiership curtain raiser three days later would be the first real test for Kevin Keegan's talented side, which featured several new signings. David Seaman, Michael Tarnat, Paul Bosvelt, Antoine Sibierski and Sinclair all made their debuts at The Valley against a side that had a habit of being a thorn in the Blues' side.

Yet a majestic display with goals for Nicolas Anelka, Jihai Sun and Sibierski swept away

the Addicks 3-0 and left the travelling fans dreaming of a wonderful ten months ahead. The first Premiership visitors to the new ground were Portsmouth and for most of the game, it looked like they would take all three points. Thankfully, David Sommeil popped up with a late goal to earn a 1-1 draw.

A fantastic 3-2 win at Blackburn saw City top the Premiership and though they lost 2-1 at home to Arsenal the following Sunday, Aston Villa became the first team to leave Eastlands with nothing as the Blues ran riot 4-1.

By mid-October, a 6-2 home win over Bolton had seen Keegan's men well-placed with Arsenal, Chelsea and Manchester United, in fourth position in the table. Defeat followed at Stamford Bridge but a rare 2-0 win at Southampton put City back into the top five.

That would be the last victory for 14 games! The team slipped out of Europe and the Coca Cola Cup and plummeted down to fifteenth position in the league. Many wondered why such a talented side were playing so badly but there were several occasions when City dominated games but still ended up losing or drawing.

Also of concern was the fact that City had won just two league games out of the opening 13 – things were getting desperate and only a 3-1 at Leicester City and a fantastic comeback against Tottenham – both in the FA Cup – relieved the growing pressure on the players.

David James had been signed from West Ham United following David Seaman's decision to retire and the England No.1 immediately made an impact with a series of impressive displays.

Yet Manchester United ended the dreams of cup success, despite being outplayed for long periods of the game, with a 4-2 win in the fifth round. Then, at last, a 3-1 win at Bolton ended a sequence of 14 games without a Premiership win. Despite playing Chelsea off the park in the next game, City lost 1-0 and were back in trouble.

Typical, then, that United had the better of the Manchester derby for long periods but it was the Blues who triumphed with an exhilarating 4-1 putting the smiles back on the fans' faces. There was still work to be done, but this result made things much easier!

Incredibly, a run of seven games followed without a win as the team failed to capitalise on the boost against the Reds and by the time Newcastle visited, the threat of relegation was all-too real.

Roared on by yet another full house, the Blues saved one of their best performances of the season until last and Paulo Wanchope, injured for much of the season, won the game with a stunning second-half header. That, coupled with Leeds' defeat at Bolton the next day, ensured Premiership survival and allowed everyone to sleep easier and start thinking of summer holidays again!

The final game, at home to Everton, saw the teams battle for the right to finish in sixteenth position. City, playing in a relaxed and confident style, won easily 5-1, playing the kind of football everyone knew they were capable of – the mystery was why they hadn't done it more often.

Joey Barton

Young midfielder Joey Barton has come a long way since famously having his shirt stolen minutes before he was set to make his debut at Middlesbrough in November 2002. As the youngster prepared to come on as a substitute at the Riverside Stadium, he discovered a fan had reached into the dugout during the half-time break and taken his jersey!

Crestfallen, the Huyton-born youngster had to wait almost five months before finally making his first appearance for the Blues in a 2-0 defeat at Bolton. Since then, he's been hard to leave out of the team and he has also become one of the most important players at the club.

Adored by the fans, who love his wholehearted, all-action style and crunching tackles, Barton has progressed through the City Academy and graduated with flying colours, especially as he was on the verge of being released!

He adds fire to the heart of the Blues' midfield but knows he has to learn to channel his aggression in the right manner and not pick up as many yellow cards as he did last season – but all that will come with experience.

Barton also won selection to the England Under-21 squad last season and scored in his second appearance at Goodison, the home of his boyhood idols Everton. He only managed one for City – a sublime effort against Blackburn Rovers – and will be looking to add more goals to his game this coming season.

He played 24 times in the Premiership in 2003/04 and added four more from the bench and was the supporters' choice for Young Player of the Year 2003. There is much more to come from this talented player.

2003/04 season stats

Date	Versus	Score	Gate	Scorers
14/08	TNS (UEFA CUP)	5-0	34,103	Sinclair, Sommeil, Sun, Anelka, Wright-Phillips
17/08	Charlton Athletic	3-0	25,780	Anelka (p), Sibierski, Sun
23/08	Portsmouth	1-1	46,287	Sommeil
25/08	Blackburn Rovers	3-2	23,361	Tarnat, Barton, Anelka
28/08	TNS (UEFA CUP)	2-0	10,123	Negouai, Huckerby
31/08	Arsenal	1-2	46,436	Lauren (og)
14/09	Aston Villa	4-1	46,687	Anelka 3 (2 p) Tarnat
20/09	Fulham	2-2	16,124	Knight (og) Wanchope
24/09	Lokeren (UEFA 1/1)	3-2	29,067	Sibierski, Fowler, Anelka (p)
28/09	Tottenham	0-0	46,842	
04/10	Wolves	0-1	29,386	
15/10	Lokeren (UEFA 1/2)	1-0	9,000	Anelka (p)
18/10	Bolton Wanderers	6-2	47,101	Wright-Phillips (2), Distin, Anelka (2), Reyna
25/10	Chelsea	0-1	41,040	
28/10	QPR (Carling Cup 3)	3-0	16,773	Wright-Phillips (2), Macken
01/11	Southampton	2-0	31,952	Fowler, Wanchope
06/11	Groclin (UEFA 2/1)	1-1	32,101	Anelka
09/11	Leicester City	0-3	46,966	
22/11	Newcastle United	0-3	52,159	
27/11	Groclin (UEFA 2/2)	0-0	5,000	
30/11	Middlesbrough	0-1	46,824	
03/12	Tottenham (Carling 4)	1-3	31,727	Fowler
06/12	Everton	0-0	37,871	
13/12	Manchester United	1-3	67,645	Wright-Phillips
22/12	Leeds United	1-1	47,126	Sibierski
26/12	Birmingham City	1-2	29,520	Fowler
28/12	Liverpool	2-2	47,201	Anelka (p), Fowler
03/01	Leicester City (FAC3)	2-2	30,617	Anelka 2 (p)
07/01	Charlton Athletic	1-1	44,307	Fowler
10/01	Portsmouth	2-4	20,120	Sibierski, Anelka
14/01	Leicester (FAC3R)	3-1	18,916	Sibierski, Anelka, Macken
17/01	Blackburn Rovers	1-1	47,090	Anelka
18/01	Tottenham (FAC4)	1-1	28,840	Anelka
01/02	Arsenal	1-2	38,103	Anelka
04/02	Tottenham (FAC4R)	4-3	30,400	Distin, Bosvelt, Wright-Phillips, Macken
08/02	Birmingham City	0-0	46,967	
11/02	Liverpool	1-2	43,257	Wright-Phillips
15/02	Manchester Utd (FAC5)	2-4	67,400	Tarnat, Fowler
21/02	Bolton Wanderers	3-1	27,301	Fowler (2), Charlton (og)
28/02	Chelsea	0-1	47,304	
14/03	Manchester United	4-1	47,284	Fowler, Macken, Sinclair, Wright-Phillips
22/03	Leeds United	1-2	36,998	Anelka
27/03	Fulham	0-0	46,522	
04/04	Aston Villa	1-1	37,602	Distin
10/04	Wolves	3-3	47,248	Anelka, Wright-Phillips, Sibierski
12/04	Tottenham	1-1	35,282	Anelka
17/04	Southampton	1-3	47,152	Anelka
24/04	Leicester City	1-1	31,457	Tarnat
01/05	Newcastle United	1-0	47,226	Wanchope
08/05	Middlesbrough	1-2	34,734	Wanchope
15/05	Everton	5-1	47,284	Wanchope 2, Anelka, Sibierski, Wright-Phillips

			Home					Away						
		P	W	D	L	F	A	W	D	L	F	A	GD	PTS
1	Arsenal	38	15	4	0	40	14	11	8	0	33	12	47	90
2	Chelsea	38	12	4	3	34	13	12	3	4	33	17	37	79
3	Man Utd	38	12	4	3	37	15	11	2	6	27	20	29	75
4	Liverpool	38	10	4	5	29	15	6	8	5	26	22	18	60
5	Newcastle	38	11	5	3	33	14	2	12	5	19	26	12	56
6	Aston Villa	38	9	6	4	24	19	6	5	8	24	25	4	56
7	Charlton	38	7	6	6	29	29	7	5	7	22	22	0	53
8	Bolton	38	6	8	5	24	21	8	3	8	24	35	-8	53
9	Fulham	38	9	4	6	29	21	5	6	8	23	25	6	52
10	Birmingham	38	8	5	6	26	24	4	9	6	17	24	-5	50
11	Middlesbrough	38	8	4	7	25	23	5	5	9	19	29	-8	48
12	Southampton	38	8	6	5	24	17	4	5	10	20	28	-1	47
13	Portsmouth	38	10	4	5	35	19	2	5	12	12	35	-7	45
14	Tottenham	38	9	4	6	33	27	4	2	13	14	30	-10	45
15	Blackburn	38	5	4	10	25	31	7	4	8	26	28	-8	44
16	**Man City**	**38**	**5**	**9**	**5**	**31**	**24**	**4**	**5**	**10**	**24**	**30**	**1**	**41**
17	Everton	38	8	5	6	27	20	1	7	11	18	37	-12	39
18	Leicester	38	3	10	6	19	28	3	5	11	29	37	-17	33
19	Leeds	38	5	7	7	25	31	3	2	14	15	48	-39	33
20	Wolverhampton	38	7	5	7	23	35	0	7	12	15	42	-39	33

Name Game

Think you're good with anagrams?
Well try and work out these City players from the jumbled words
below. Get yourself a piece of paper, a pencil and have patience!

1. Sam Jive Dad

2. You're a Nice Lad

3. A Sister Onion Bike

4. Rail Corn Strive

5. Pub Slave Lot

6. Cave Man Stem Man

7. The Rust Gave Lard Liken

8. Visit Inns Lady

9. The Rat Bench

10. Dive Greeter Leg

Location, Location Quiz

All the questions below are on current City players – test your knowledge to the maximum or simply deduce who the individual is…

1. Which player was born in Welwyn Garden City in 1970?

2. Who was born in Versailles, France in 1979?

3. Who was born in Huyton in 1982?

4. Which player was born in Swindon in 1975 but now represents Wales?

5. What birthplace do Richard Dunne, Paddy McCarthy and Willo Flood share?

6. Who has lived in New Jersey, Germany and Glasgow?

7. Who was born in Bagnolet, France in 1977?

8. Who was born in a place called Dalian?

9. Can you name the City star who was born in Dulwich?

10. Which City defender was born in Warrington?

The Boss

If you asked Kevin Keegan which has been his favourite season as a manager, chances are he would say the 2003/04 campaign was particularly high on his list. The Blues' boss kept a smile on his face but at times it must have been hard to give interviews, especially during a long run of games without a win.

Things turned out okay in the end but, like every other City fan, he must have been glad to see the back of last season. And yet things had started so brightly – one defeat in ten and all the new signings starting off well, he must have thought that his hopes of a top six Premiership finish and maybe a good run in a cup competition were well on course.

It didn't turn out that way and by the time David Seaman announced his retirement in January, Keegan must have reckoned he'd run over a black cat without realising it!

But the New Year brought renewed hope and it was a masterstroke to bring David James to the club during the transfer window.

The Blues gradually began to find their form again, thanks to some stunning victories in the FA Cup and finally a win at Bolton relieved the growing pressure on the team. Then KK had to have hospital treatment for a painful back that resulted in him missing four games – all of which were drawn!

City then did enough in the closing weeks to survive but the manager was far from happy with the team's under-achievement last term and will be demanding a much-improved season this year.

The one thing the boss was happy with was the way the City fans backed the team despite the poor form and teething problems at the City of Manchester Stadium. With everyone pulling together, there is no reason why last season's lofty expectations cannot be met this year instead.

Nico's 24 Carat Goals

Nicolas Anelka was again City's top scorer last season with an impressive 24 strikes to his name. This is how they went in…

1.   v TNS (Aug)   87 mins
GOAL!! Anelka fires a shot in from the right, which the goalkeeper is too slow to get down to and the ball flies in off the underside of Doherty's body.

2.   v Charlton (Aug)   13 mins
GOAL!! Scott Parker pushes Shaun Wright-Phillips in the penalty area and referee awards City a penalty. Anelka calmly strokes the ball home for City's first Premiership goal of the new season.

3.   v Blackburn (Aug)   87 mins
GOAL!! A long clearance from defence found Anelka on his own inside the Blackburn box. The French striker took the ball to the right where with the deftest of touches he nutmegged the keeper to win the game and put City top.

4.   v Aston Villa (Sept)   48 mins
GOAL!! The first of three goals in this game came as a result of a penalty after Steve McManaman dribbled into the area but the ball was handled by Alpay. Anelka stepped up and coolly placed the ball low to the right hand corner beyond Thomas Sorenson.

5.   v Aston Villa (Sept)   68 mins
Jihai Sun was brought down by Peter Whittingham and referee Halsey pointed to the spot. Nicolas Anelka drove the ball to the left hand side of the net for his second of the afternoon.

6.   v Aston Villa (Sept)   83 mins
Nico grabbed his hat-trick with a wonderful solo effort when he ran from deep, drew the Villa defence towards him before planting a low shot to the left hand corner to secure the deserved win and the match ball.

7.   v Lokeren (Sept)   80 mins
Sun made an excellent breaking run down the right but was felled in the box by a defender. Up stepped Anelka who casually blasted the ball into the corner of the net.

8.   v Lokeren (Oct)   19 mins
Anelka stroked home his fifth penalty of the season after Paulo Wanchope was fouled as he rose to try and connect with Michael Tarnat's cross.

9.   v Bolton (Oct)   58 mins
Sibierski sent through Anelka who headed for the left hand side of the Bolton box and let rip with a shot that beat Jaaskelainen at his near post.

10.   v Bolton (Oct)   72 mins
Tiatto spotted a clever run from Anelka who then took the ball into the area and coolly slotted home past a sprawling Jaaskelainen.

11.   v Groclin (Nov) 6 mins
Robbie Fowler spotted a gaping hole in the Groclin defence and picked out Anelka's run down the middle. The prolific Frenchman then coolly lobbed the on-rushing keeper.

12.   v Liverpool (Dec)   30 mins
Tarnat whipped in a corner and the referee spotted an infringement on Fowler and gave a penalty. Anelka stepped up and comfortably slotted the ball past Dudek to end a run of ten games without a goal.

13.   v Leicester City (Jan)   27 mins
McKinley brought down Paul Bosvelt just inside the box resulting in a penalty for the home side. Nicolas Anelka made no mistake when he slotted the ball past Walker.

14. v Leicester City (Jan)   69 mins
Fowler whipped in a corner and Anelka towered high above the defence to nod the ball over the fingertips of Walker. Only his second headed goal in English football.

15. v Portsmouth (Jan)   21 mins
Sibierski provided a cross from the left to the corner of the penalty area where Trevor Sinclair headed the ball into the path of the French striker. His sweetly struck volley, perhaps his best of the season, was also his fiftieth goal in the Premiership.

16. v Leicester City (Jan)   90 mins
A real poacher's goal - defender Frank Sinclair tried to shield the ball back to his goalkeeper but Anelka got a foot to the ball to guide it into the left hand corner of the net.

17. v Blackburn (Jan)   50 mins
Anelka scored a wonderful curling free kick from just outside the area after Bosvelt had been brought down with a clumsy challenge. The Frenchman bent it past the outstretched Friedel for a delightful goal.

18. v Tottenham (Jan)   11 mins
Tarnat curled in a wonderful cross that Dunne nodded to Distin who in turn headed to Fowler who then hit the left post. Anelka was on the prowl and pounced from five yards out to knock the rebound into the back of the net.

19. v Arsenal (Feb)   89 mins
Another goal at Highbury for Anelka who finished off a nice move with a low drive but was then sent off in the fracas that followed!

20. v Leeds (Mar)   44 mins
Sibierski cleverly slotted the ball through to Anelka via a deft back heel and the French striker obliged by firing home a wonderful shot.

21. v Wolves (Apr)   25 mins
Anelka rose and hung in the air to head the ball onto the post and into the net from a Tarnat cross.

22. v Tottenham (Apr)   25 mins
Steve McManaman provided the initial pass just inside the area. Spurs defender Doherty missed his tackle on the French striker and Nico's neat footwork did the rest as he stroked the ball home.

23. v Southampton (Apr)   78 mins
No more than a consolation effort in a miserable home defeat.

24. v Everton (May)   41 mins
Nico took the ball along the edge of the area and, with the Everton defence holding off, he beautifully placed the ball low with his left foot to the corner of the net.

Which Team?

Here's a real test of how much you know about the City players.
Can you name which player supported which club when they were kids?

1. **Joey Barton supported:**
   a) Liverpool b) Everton c) Tranmere

2. **Robbie Fowler supported:**
   a) Everton b) Leeds United c) Liverpool

3. **Shaun Wright-Phillips supported:**
   a) Nottingham Forest b) Arsenal c) Tottenham

4. **Steve McManaman supported:**
   a) Manchester United b) Everton c) Liverpool

5. **Nick Weaver supported:**
   a) Sheffield United b) Leeds United c) Sheffield Weds

6. **Trevor Sinclair supported:**
   a) QPR b) West Brom c) Manchester City

7. **Jon Macken supported:**
   a) Burnley b) Manchester City c) Oldham Athletic

8. **Ben Thatcher supported:**
   a) Swindon b) Southampton c) Millwall

9. **Stephen Jordan supported:**
   a) Everton b) Manchester City c) Leicester City

10. **Bradley Wright-Phillips supported:**
    a) Arsenal b) Millwall c) Notts County

Guess Who

1.

2.

3.

4.

5.

Last Man Standing

David James is the last line of defence for both City and England and he performs both jobs admirably. He joined City last January from West Ham and played 17 games from then until the end of the season, with the Blues losing six times in that run and just about preserving their top-flight status.

Many reckoned it was James' influence on the defence that saved the club from relegation and he made several spectacular saves, notably at Bolton and at home to Wolves. But it was two crucial penalty saves against Wolves and Leicester that made James an instant hero with the supporters.

Each of those games were level when the spot-kicks were awarded and had they gone in, City may well have gone into the last game of the season needing a win to have any chance of staying up, but the matches both yielded a point and by the time the Blues travelled to Middlesbrough on the penultimate Saturday, they were safe.

Now James is looking forward to starting the new season with a clean slate and stabilising a position that saw no less than six goalkeepers feature for the Blues last season - David Seaman, Kevin Ellegaard, Arni Arason, Kasper Schmeichel and Nicky Weaver being the other five.

James is also England's No.1 choice and played all four games at Euro 2004 when, ironically, the penalty specialist just couldn't get near the Portuguese kicks in the penalty-shoot out in the quarter-final. Though Chris Kirkland and Paul Robinson are waiting in the wings, it's likely James will still be in goal for the World Cup in Germany – as long as England qualify!

James began his career at Watford where he played 89 times over a four-year period. He then moved to Liverpool and remained at Anfield for seven seasons, making 214 appearances for them. Two seasons at Aston Villa followed his stint on Merseyside before he was off back to London with West Ham United.

Happy though he was at Upton Park, the Hammers had slipped into Division One and the National goalkeeper had to be playing Premiership football to be in with a chance of keeping his place, so when Kevin Keegan offered him the opportunity to replace the retiring David Seaman, he jumped at the chance.

A keen artist and DJ away from football, James follows in a long tradition of great City goalkeepers. Tony Coton, Joe Corrigan, Harry Dowd, Bert Trautmann and Frank Swift are just some of his illustrious predecessors – if he is mentioned in the same breath as any of those names, he will have had a long and successful career at the City of Manchester Stadium.

True or False?

1. City boss Kevin Keegan was twice voted European Player of the Year. True or False?

2. Coach Stuart Pearce was training to be an electrician before he became a professional footballer. True or False?

3. City were once relegated from Division One the season after winning it. True or False?

4. Claudio Reyna was the first American to play for City. True or False?

5. Musicians New Order, Oasis, Badly Drawn Boy and The Doves are all huge City fans. True or False?

6. City once lost to Chelsea 5-4 at Wembley. True or False?

7. More than 1 million fans passed through the turnstiles at the City of Manchester Stadium last season. True or False?

8. Nicolas Anelka holds the record for most penalties scored for the Blues in one season. True or False?

9. City were the first team to win the League Cup. True or False?

10. Michael Owen was a City youth team player before he joined Liverpool. True or False?

Don't Quote Me

Who said the following last season?

1. "When I scored against Aston Villa they kept shouting 'Shoot! Shoot! Every time I got the ball and because my English was not so good, I thought they were booing me!"

2. "If there is a positive about being at home more than I would normally, it is being able to spend more time with my baby. I've been able to watch her grow and been able to play with her more often."

3. "I don't read the papers, I leave that to my friends. They ring me up and tell me whenever anything has been said about me."

4. "I'd like to play for an American team for a couple of years and where we settle maybe be linked to the area that team play in."

5. "The City fans have made me feel at home from the word go with the reception against Blackburn. If that's anything to go by and we can improve on that, then we're all going to be very happy."

6. "Although Liverpool is only 30 miles away, I found it quite difficult to settle when I first signed for the club. I have got used to the drive over now and I feel settled and that is showing through in my football."

7. "I've always felt at home in England. I came here to play football – not just for the nice weather!"

8. "What do you want him to do? Six cartwheels and a somersault? I don't care what he does, as long as he scores."

9. "In the beginning it was not hard exactly but I don't like to shout – I am not that kind of player."

10. "As far as me being famous, that's tough for me to answer. There were an awful lot of people who watched me in a few live games but I don't know if that's anything to gauge my popularity by."

Three Lions Come Home

England played their first games at the City of Manchester Stadium last summer against Japan and Iceland in the FA Summer Tournament. England drew the first game 1-1 with Japan but won the second game 6-1 against Iceland. Here is a selection of pictures from these historic games.

The Greatest Comeback...Ever!

They call football a game of two halves and this was the game that proved it to be true. It was a match that will be remembered and talked about for many years to come. But for so long, it looked likely to be a game that every City fan would want to forget!

The FA Cup draw matched the Blues with one of their traditional cup rivals. The teams had met many times before in both the League and FA Cups and Tottenham definitely held the upper hand and had already knocked City out of the Coca-Cola Cup earlier in the season. They also beat the Blues in the 1981 FA Cup final after a replay.

The teams drew 1-1 at the City of Manchester Stadium in the original fourth round tie with City dominating the first half but Spurs controlled the second period. The replay at White Hart Lane would be exactly the opposite.

Things looked bad for City when Ledley King put the home side ahead after just two minutes. Robbie Keane made it 2-0 and then leading scorer Nicolas Anelka limped off injured. Right on the stroke of half time, Christian Ziege scored a terrific free kick to give the home side a 3-0 lead. Before the teams even reached the dressing rooms, things got even worse for the Blues!

Joey Barton, who had already been booked, questioned a decision by referee Rob Styles and was shown the red card. Down to ten men, 3-0 down and the leading scorer off injured – it couldn't get any worse.

Kevin Keegan asked his team to go and show some pride but deep down, he must have thought this was going to be his heaviest defeat as City boss. If City, quoted at 250-1 to win from this position, were to have any hope, they had to score straight away – and they did. A chipped free kick from Michael Tarnat found Sylvain Distin who headed home for 3-1. Then, Spurs almost went 4-1 ahead. Another Ziege free kick was pushed on to the bar by Arni Arason, making his debut, but the ball fell to Gus Poyet who had to score. He headed towards an empty goal only to see Arason make a wonderful recovery and grasp the ball on the line.

Then Paul Bosvelt sent in a shot that was deflected past Kasey Keller for 3-2. City couldn't really come back could they? Around 2000 travelling Blues and many thousands watching the game live on television certainly hoped so!

With the clock ticking down, Shaun Wright-Phillips attacked the home defence and he finished his run with a delightful chip over Keller for 3-3. The City fans in the ground – and at home – went wild. But there was more to come. With time almost up, Tarnat picked the ball up on the left, looked up and saw Jon Macken in the box. His perfect cross was met with a firm header by Macken and the ball sailed past Keller for a dramatic, incredible last minute winner.

It was one of the best City performances in living memory and one of the greatest – if not **the** greatest – come-backs ever. Well done lads!

Player Profiles

David James

Capped 25 times by his country, David James joined City from West Ham United in January 2004. James established himself as England's first choice when former City 'keeper David Seaman ended his 13-year reign as No.1. His arrival at Manchester City helped steady the defence and he made a number of crucial saves, including two penalty stops, which undoubtedly helped save the club from relegation.

Geert de Vlieger

Belgian international goalkeeper Geert de Vlieger joined City from Dutch club Willem II in the close season as a replacement for Arni Arason. De Vlieger represented his country in the 2002 World Cup and will be hoping to push David James hard for a place in the starting line-up.

Nicky Weaver

Now the longest serving player at City, Weaver has missed the best part of three seasons through injury. His last operation, it is hoped, should cure the problem once and for all and allow the unlucky goalkeeper to resume his promising career.

Kevin Ellegaard

The young Danish goalkeeper was thrust into the first team following injuries to Seaman and Weaver and was unfortunate to play in a side short on confidence. He looked more assured each game and will have benefited tremendously from his first team experience.

Ben Thatcher

Ben Thatcher signed for City in the summer and the tough tackling left back will replace Michael Tarnat who left the club at the end of last season. Thatcher began life at Millwall before being transferred to Wimbledon for £2.1m. He spent several seasons with the Dons before signing for Tottenham for £5m. Injuries restricted his progress at White Hart Lane and last season he signed for Leicester City. A Welsh international, Thatcher will wear the No.3 shirt this season.

Richard Dunne

One of the success stories of last season, Dunne fought his way back into the first team early on and remained there for the rest of the campaign. His consistency and solid defending earned him runners-up spot in the Player of the Year award and ensured he would be an automatic choice for the new season.

Player Profiles

David Sommeil

After spending half a season with Marseille, David Sommeil has returned to City to challenge for a place in the back four. Sommeil and Daniel van Buyten had swapped clubs for a few months but van Buyten's move to Hamburg scuppered a permanent move to Marseille for Sommeil who will be keen to impress the manager and win back his place in the first team.

Sylvain Distin

The Blues' captain had to adjust to leading the team last season but appeared to be far more comfortable towards the end of the 2003/04 campaign than he was at the beginning. A naturally quiet person, Distin had to learn to become more vocal out on the pitch. He was the only City player to play every minute of every Premiership game last season and also scored his first goals for the club, too.

Stephen Jordan

Jordan signed a new one-year deal with the Blues and will be first choice cover for new signing Ben Thatcher. The young left back has had limited first team opportunities so far and will be hoping to break into the team at some point this campaign.

Paddy McCarthy

Young Ireland centre-half Paddy McCarthy was given a vote of confidence by Kevin Keegan when he told the defender he'd moved ahead of Mikkel Bischoff in the queue for first team football. An old fashioned, physical player, McCarthy should feature at some point in 2004/05.

Jihai Sun

Like most of the defenders at the club, Jihai Sun will be glad to begin with a clean slate this season. Sun played the majority of the campaign as first choice right back and began with two goals in the first two games – but then failed to score again all season! He provided valuable support to the City attack, winning several penalties and also providing a number of quality crosses.

Paul Bosvelt

Dutch midfielder Paul Bosvelt provided much-needed experience in the middle of the park last season and linked up well with Joey Barton in a number of games. Part of the Euro 2004 Holland squad, Bosvelt enjoys both the anchor role in front of the defence or supporting the attack, though his only goal was a deflected shot away to Tottenham!

Player Profiles

Steve McManaman

The former Real Madrid and Liverpool star made a stunning debut against Aston Villa last season but injuries restricted his appearances and he never really enjoyed a long run in the first team. Will be keen to rediscover the kind of form that made him an England regular a few years back and also still looking for his first goal in City colours.

Antoine Sibierski

Attacking midfielder Antoine Sibierski was signed from Lens in time for the start of the 2003/04 season in a deal worth £700,000. The French star provided valuable support to the strikers and was a constant threat from set-pieces, scoring six goals in total and could have maybe doubled that amount with a bit more luck!

Claudio Reyna

American international Claudio Reyna signed for City from Sunderland in September 2003 for £2.5m. The former Glasgow Rangers and Bayer Leverkusen star has earned more than 100 caps for his country – one of only six Americans to have reached the landmark and has played in two World Cup tournaments.

Trevor Sinclair

When both City and Middlesbrough tabled bids for Trevor Sinclair, there was only one team he would choose. Sinclair, raised in Manchester, was a City fan as a boy and his move from West Ham enabled him to realise a lifelong ambition and play for the Blues. Scored the first competitive goal at the new stadium and also came off the bench to score a crucial goal against Manchester United.

Mikkel Bischoff

Dogged by injury since his move to City, Mikkel Bischoff has made just three starts in three years at the club. The classy central defender has long been tagged as 'one to watch' but will surely need to steer clear of injury this season to have any chance of making it with City. With a bit more luck, he could soon be pushing for first team football.

Joey Barton

Joey Barton's rise to prominence at City has been nothing short of remarkable considering the young Merseysider was almost released by the club a couple of years back. Now starting just his second full season at first team level, he is a firm favourite with the fans and the perfect example of what hard work and persistence can achieve. He will get better and better.

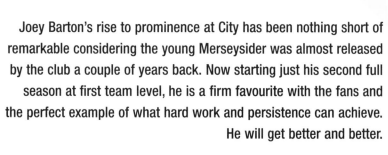

Player Profiles

Shaun Wright-Phillips

City's Player of the Year for 2004 after winning the young players' award for the previous three, Shaun Wright-Phillips is the darling of the Manchester City fans. Wholehearted and totally committed, Wright-Phillips was the star of the 2003/04 season with a series of fantastic performances and spectacular goals. Also won international recognition and will surely feature in the World Cup qualifiers this year.

Jon Macken

Limited first team opportunities since his £5.5m move from Preston North End, mainly due to injury problems, but looks to be fit and ready to challenge for a regular starting place after several impressive starts last term. His strengths are holding the ball up and, given the chance, he is an excellent finisher. Will be desperate to force his way into the reckoning this season.

Paulo Wanchope

Finished last season with a flurry of goals and looks set to be first choice partner to Nicolas Anelka for the new season. With just 51 League starts out of a possible 160 in his first four seasons, Wanchope has been robbed of almost three years of first team football but after a successful knee operation, it seems the talented Costa Rican can at last progress with his career.

Bradley Wright-Phillips

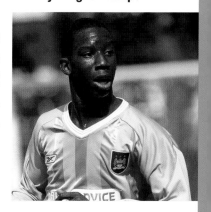

Younger brother of Shaun, Bradley won rave reviews for his scoring exploits in the reserves last season. Like his adopted dad Ian Wright, Bradley looks a natural finisher and with the departure of Stephen Elliott, has moved up a slot in the battle for first team football. Expect to see him figure in the first team squad this season.

Robbie Fowler

Though the Toxteth Terror hasn't rediscovered the kind of form that made him a legend at Liverpool, Fowler has showed flashes of his old self and managed to reach double figures in goals in his first full season with the Blues. Will need to be at his best to win a place in the starting line up but has the ability and instinct to score 20 goals if he hits form.

Nicolas Anelka

The French superstar again finished top scorer for the Blues in his second season at City and will be the favourite to do the same again in 2004/05. Though the subject of constant transfer speculation, Anelka has always claimed to be happy at City and will be hoping for a recall to the French squad following this season.

Academy Prospects

City has a wonderful tradition of finding young talent and that reputation looks set to continue for many years to come. In the 1960s there was Alan Oakes, Mike Doyle, Tommy Booth, Glyn Pardoe and Neil Young. In the 1970s there was Peter Barnes, Gary Owen, Clive Wilson, Nicky Reid and Ray Ranson. The 1980s was particularly successful with Ian Brightwell, Paul Moulden, David White, Paul Simpson, Paul Lake and Steve Redmond breaking into the first team and the 1990s saw the likes of Garry Flitcroft and Steve Lomas emerge.

Recent discoveries have been Shaun Wright-Phillips and Joey Barton and there are others set to follow. Shaun's younger brother Bradley Wright-Phillips will be looking to continue scoring in the reserves this season and defender Paddy McCarthy looks set to break into the first team before long. The selling of a number of fringe first team players means that youngsters will be able to be tested in the reserves and gain valuable experience.

Both the Under 17s and the Under 19s had excellent seasons last year and there are a number of players who have caught the eye. Lee Croft has played at almost every level for England bar the Under 21s and seniors and he will be expected to push hard for the first team squad. Nedum Onouha and the D'Laryea brothers have progressed extremely well and Ishmael Miller will be looking to continue the fine scoring form of 2003/04.

Elsewhere, winger Jamie Tandy and left-back Paul Collins had good campaigns with the Under 19s and are both highly rated and expect to hear a lot of the exciting Kelvin Etuhu, brother of former City star Dickson, and Danny Sturridge in 2005.

The success of the Academy is down to the excellent coaching staff at Platt Lane, headed by Jim Cassell. Alex Gibson, Frankie Bunn and Paul Power are all helping shape the young Blues of tomorrow and saving the club millions of pound in the process. The age groups will change next season with the two main Academy teams being the Under 16s and the Under 18s.

The home games are played at Platt Lane on Saturday mornings and support is always welcome.

Player Stats & City Career
League Only

Player	Appearances 2003/04	Goals	Appearances City Career	Goals
David James	17	0	17	0
Kevin Stuhr-Ellegaard	2 (2)	0	2 (2)	0
Geert de Vlieger	-	-	-	-
Nicky Weaver	1	0	145 (1)	0
Sun Jihai	30 (4)	2	56 (12)	3
Richard Dunne	28 (1)	0	117 (5)	1
Ben Thatcher	-	-	-	-
Joey Barton	24 (4)	1	31 (4)	2
Paul Bosvelt	22 (3)	0	22 (3)	0
Sylvain Distin	38	3	72	2
Steve McManaman	20 (2)	0	20 (2)	0
Claudio Reyna	19 (4)	1	19 (4)	1
Antoine Sibierski	18 (14)	5	18 (4)	5
David Sommeil	18	1		
Shaun Wright-Phillips	32 (2)	7	97 (22)	16
Paulo Wanchope	12 (10)	6	51 (13)	27
Jonathan Macken	7 (8)	1	11 (17)	7
Robbie Fowler	23 (8)	7	35 (9)	9
Nicolas Anelka	31 (1)	17	69 (1)	30
Stephen Jordan	0 (2)	0	0 (3)	0
Trevor Sinclair	20 (9)	1	20 (9)	1

City Edge Premiership Derby Honours

With Manchester United still smarting from gaining just one point in the last season's Manchester derbies, City made their way warily to Old Trafford for the first clash in December last year. The Blues played poorly and when United raced 2-0 ahead, it looked like it could be a bad day for the Blue half of the city. Despite under-performing, City came out after the break with renewed vigour and Shaun Wright-Phillips scored a wonderful solo goal to make it 2-1. Robbie Fowler came close with a spectacular long-range header but it was the home side that scored next and won 3-1.

City's reward for the comeback of the decade at Tottenham, was a FA Cup 5th round tie at Old Trafford. United took the lead but City were well on top and, when Gary Neville was red carded for a clash of heads with Steve McManaman, things looked good for Keegan's side. For 20 minutes the Blues battered United with Joey Barton, McManaman and Fowler all going close, but it just wasn't to be and United broke twice to go 3-0 ahead. Despite goals from Michael Tarnat and Fowler, United won 4-2 and went on to win the FA Cup.

When the teams met for the first ever derby at the new stadium, it was City's turn to smile as they quickly went 2-0 up through Fowler and Jon Macken. Scholes replied for United but substitute Trevor Sinclair sent hundreds of Reds heading for the exit when he nipped in to make it 3-1 in the second half. But the best was yet to come, the United fans, who had taunted the City supporters twice at Old Trafford in the preceding months, sat silently – those who hadn't left – as the clock ticked over 90 minutes. Then, Shaun Wright-Phillips broke down the right. As he neared the area, he decided to have a crack at goal and the ball flew in off the underside of the bar to send the home fans wild. The 4-1 win was the biggest over United since September 1989 when City triumphed 5-1.

The United fans who claimed to have buried some of their team's shirts under the new stadium and then issued a curse left with egg on their faces for the second year running. United may have won two out of the three clashes, but it felt like City had definitely had the last laugh!

City Stadium Rocks!

The City of Manchester Stadium began life as the venue for the 2002 Commonwealth Games before being dramatically altered to a football arena and ready to become the new home of Manchester City in August 2003.

But it's not just football that the stadium will be used for and 2004 saw two prime examples of its versatility. In June, Californian rockers Red Hot Chili Peppers played on the pitch after 60,000 tickets were sold in a matter of hours. City's old ground, Maine Road, hosted many top bands down the years and there will be more concerts in the future.

Rugby League will be the second sport to feature at the stadium when Great Britain and Australia play as part of the Gillette Tri-Nations Tournament. There is also the added attraction of the new 180 foot sculpture The B of the Bang now on display outside the stadium and a new hotel being built - the Blues' home is certainly the place to be.

City's reserve side will play their home games alongside the senior's home when they take residence of the adjacent athletics stadium – a move that is likely to see the second string's crowds double.

As the Chili Peppers proved, the City of Manchester Stadium is a stadium to be rocked!

Who am I?

1. I was born in England and began life with Millwall. I went to the Lileshall School of Excellence where I studied Kenny Sansom and Stuart Pearce's techniques. I've played for the England Under 21s but now represent Wales Who am I?

2. At a former club, I once scored five goals in one game and I hold the record for the quickest hat-trick in the Premiership – 4 minutes and 22 seconds. I scored my first goal for City against Birmingham Who am I?

3. I was born in Warrington and have been with City since I was at school. I made my debut at Bolton but my haircut seemed to cause quite a stir. I made my home debut against Everton Who am I?

4. I was born in Doncaster but began my career at Scunthorpe. I have played for Newcastle and Southampton and have also played abroad Who am I?

5. I began my career at Manchester United but signed for another north-west team where I made a name for myself scoring goals. I once scored a goal from almost the halfway line against City before signing for the Blues in 2002 Who am I?

6. I've played for the England Under 21s and signed for City after just one game for my former club. I've been involved in a penalty shoot-out at Wembley and am now the club's longest serving player Who am I?

7. My career began many thousands of miles away and my first club was Crystal Palace. I returned home for a short spell before being the first person from my country to sign for City Who am I?

8. I've lifted the UEFA Cup at my former club and represented my country at international level. I enjoy fishing and like motorbikes Who am I?

9. I once scored a fantastic goal at Old Trafford and scored three on my home debut for City. I've scored a goal against Brazil Who am I?

10. My father is Argentinean and I began my career in Germany. I've played in the World Cup and earned over 100 caps for my country and have also played for Glasgow Rangers Who am I?

History Quiz

Think you know everything you need to know about City – then answer the questions below!

1. How many times have City been League champions in the top division?

2. How many times have City won the FA Cup?

3. Who was captain when City won the League Cup in 1976 and whom did they beat?

4. In the 1998 play off final, who scored City's penalties in the shoot-out?

5. Name the two Premiership clubs who played at the Millennium Stadium and didn't win a trophy last season.

6. What do Trevor Sinclair, Ian Bishop and Stuart Pearce all have in common?

7. What is the record transfer fee received by City and who was the player?

8. Who were the last twins to play first team football for City?

9. City were the last team to win the League championship with 11 English players. True or False?

10. Who scored the first ever and last ever goals at Maine Road for City?

Tough Enough!

Danny Mills and Ben Thatcher are two tough, uncompromising defenders who will add a touch of steel to City's defensive line this season. The pair are both established internationals for their countries – Mills for England and Thatcher for Wales and are at the peak of their careers and both signed from clubs who were relegated from the Premiership last season.

Mills began life with his boyhood club Norwich City before eventually moving on to Charlton Athletic for £250,000 and remained an Addick for several seasons before Leeds United paid £4.5 million for his services in 1999. Despite a rocky start to life at Elland Road, Mills established himself in the team and was called into the England squad, earning his first cap against Mexico.

He then continued in the national side and played every minute of England's World Cup matches in Japan and Korea. Leeds' off-field problems led to Mills being loaned out to Middlesbrough during the 2003/04 campaign but despite impressing at the Riverside Stadium, he returned to Leeds in the summer.

With the Yorkshire outfit facing life in Division One this season, they were forced to trim their wage bill and that meant Mills could leave for free. When City moved in, he quickly agreed terms and signed a five-year contract and he will begin the 2004/05 season as first choice right back.

Ben Thatcher started out his career at Millwall and made 90 appearances for them from 1993 to 1996. He was then signed by Wimbledon for a hefty £2.1million and became a firm favourite with the Dons' fans, remaining with them for four seasons before Tottenham splashed out £5.5 million in 2000. He'd by this time won an England Under-21 cap but a bad injury and a failure to see eye to eye with new manager Glenn Hoddle meant that his place in the team was usually restricted to the odd match here and there. When Leicester City offered him the chance of first team football in 2003, he jumped at the chance.

Realising his chances of playing for England were slim, Thatcher decided to exploit a new ruling that allowed him to play for another country as he had never won a full cap for England. He chose Wales and was selected to play shortly after. Ironically, the Swindon-born left back used to study videos of his boyhood hero Stuart Pearce when he was making his way in the game and now he will be learning directly from the man himself!

One thing is for sure, with Mills and Thatcher in City's defence, there are bound to be a large number of forwards nursing bruised shins from crunching tackles from the Blues' new full-backs.

Know Your History!

City opened their doors to the 'Manchester City Experience' in early 2004 offering fans a chance to visit Britain's most stunning new stadium and experience the atmosphere with unique tours and glimpses into the rarely seen world of the players.

A complete Experience tour begins with the fabulous museum, which encapsulates the club's 130-year history and the fanaticism that it has inspired. You can try your hand at being the next John Motson by commentating on glorious goals from City's past, relive the greatest moments on the Video Jukebox, or simply spend your time examining some of the club's extensive memorabilia.

There is loads of interactive stuff and even a viewing room showing videos and goals from the past.

Then, soak up the atmosphere with a behind-the-scenes tour of the City of Manchester Stadium. The guide will give you an insight into the day-to-day activities of the club, allowing you to discover what really goes on behind closed doors! Walk in the footsteps of your favourite players or admire the grandeur of the building from one of the executive lounges.

The Experience offers you the chance to share in the very special history and atmosphere of Manchester City and revel in the past, present and future of the Blues.

The Manchester City Experience is open every day except matchdays (or when any other significant event is taking place in the stadium).

Monday 11.30 to 4.30
Tuesday to Saturday 9.30 to 4.30
Sunday & Bank Holidays 11.00 to 3.00

2004/05 Prices
£7.50 (adults)
£4.50 (concessions)

Bookings can be made by calling

0870 062 1894

Further details can be obtained by emailing
experience@mcfc.co.uk

Club Honours & Awards

Football League (after 1992)
Division 1
Champions: 2001-2002
Runners up: 1999-2000
Division 2
Play Off winners: 1998-99 (Div. 2)

Football League (before 1992)
Division 1
Champions: 1936-37, 1967-68
Runners up: 1903-04, 1920-21, 1976-77
Division 2
Champions: 1898-99, 1902-03, 1909-10,
1927-28, 1946-47, 1965-66
Runners up: 1895-96, 1950-51, 1988-89

FA Cup
Winners: 1904, 1934, 1956, 1969
Runners up: 1926, 1933, 1955, 1981

League Cup
Winners: 1970, 1976
Runners up: 1974

Full Members' Cup
Runners up: 1986

European Cup Winners' Cup
Winners: 1970

Charity Shield
Winners: 1937, 1968, 1972
Runners up: 1934, 1956, 1969,1973

FA Youth Cup
Winners: 1986
Runners up: 1979, 1980, 1989

Footballer of the Year
Don Revie 1954-55
Bert Trautmann 1955-56
Tony Book 1968-69
(shared with Dave Mackay)

PFA Merit Award
Dennis Law 1975
Joe Mercer OBE 1982
Tommy Hutchinson 1992

PFA Young Player of the Year
Peter Barnes 1974-75

Answers Page

History

1 Twice – 1936/37 & 1967/68
2 Four times – 1904, 1934, 1956 & 1969
3 Mike Doyle & Newcastle
4 Kevin Horlock, Terry Cooke & Richard Edghill
5 Bolton (Coca-Cola Cup final) Manchester City
   (v TNS, UEFA Cup)
6 They all joined City from West Ham United
7 £5.5 million for Gio Kinkladze
8 The Futcher Twins, Ron and Paul in 1979
9 True, in 1967/68
10 Horace Barnes & Marc Vivien Foe

Who am I?

1 Ben Thatcher
2 Robbie Fowler
3 Stephen Jordan
4 Kevin Keegan
5 Jon Macken
6 Nick Weaver
7 Jihai Sun
8 Paul Bosvelt
9 Paulo Wanchope
10 Claudio Reyna

Location, Location

1 David James
2 Nicolas Anelka
3 Joey Barton
4 Ben Thatcher
5 Dublin
6 Claudio Reyna
7 Sylvain Distin
8 Jihai Sun
9 Trevor Sinclair
10 Stephen Jordan

Which Team?

1 Joey Barton supported: **b) Everton**
2 Robbie Fowler supported: **a) Everton**
3 Shaun Wright-Phillips supported: **b) Arsenal**
4 Steve McManaman supported: **b) Everton**
5 Nick Weaver supported: **c) Sheffield Weds**
6 Trevor Sinclair supported: **c) Manchester City**
7 Jon Macken supported: **b) Manchester City**
8 Ben Thatcher supported: **c) Millwall**
9 Stephen Jordan supported: **b) Manchester City**
10 Bradley Wright-Phillips supported: **a) Arsenal**

Guess Who

1 Trevor Sinclair
2 Steve McManaman
3 Antoine Sibierski
4 Robbie Fowler
5 Michael Tarnat

Don't Quote Me

1 Michael Tarnat
2 Paulo Wanchope
3 Shaun Wright-Phillips
4 Claudio Reyna
5 David James
6 Robbie Fowler
7 Paul Bosvelt
8 Kevin Keegan (regarding Anelka)
9 Sylvain Distin
10 Jihai Sun

True or False?

1 True
2 True
3 True
4 False – it was Gerry Baker
5 False – New Order support Manchester United
6 True – in the 1986 Full Members Cup final
7 True
8 False – Francis Lee holds the record of 15
   in 1971/72
9 False
10 False

Name Game

1 David James
2 Claudio Reyna
3 Antoine Sibierski
4 Trevor Sinclair
5 Paul Bosvelt
6 Steve McManaman
7 Kevin Stuhr Ellegaard
8 Sylvain Distin
9 Ben Thatcher
10 Geert de Vlieger